Magical Baby

ISBN: 978-1-953993-65-6

To King Maximus Chrispin

You are the best teacher a coach could ask for. I'm so proud to be your mother.

Dear Mom-to-be,

Pregnancy is a time of preparation, excitement, and anticipation. The nine months of pregnancy give you a level of connection with your unborn baby through your soothing words, your touch, and your emotions.

This beautiful book brings together soothing words that an unborn baby will love to hear and that will instantly connect them with you.

The early relationship you and your partner have with your baby during pregnancy is important. How you meet their needs and care for them shapes their brain development. This is true before they are born and when they arrive.

"Before I formed you in the womb I knew you, before you were born I
set you apart; I appointed you as a prophet to the nation."

Jeremiah 1:5

A mother's joy begins when new life is stirring inside... when a tiny heartbeat is heard for the very first time, and a playful kick reminds her that she is never alone.

-

Paper Heart family

Love

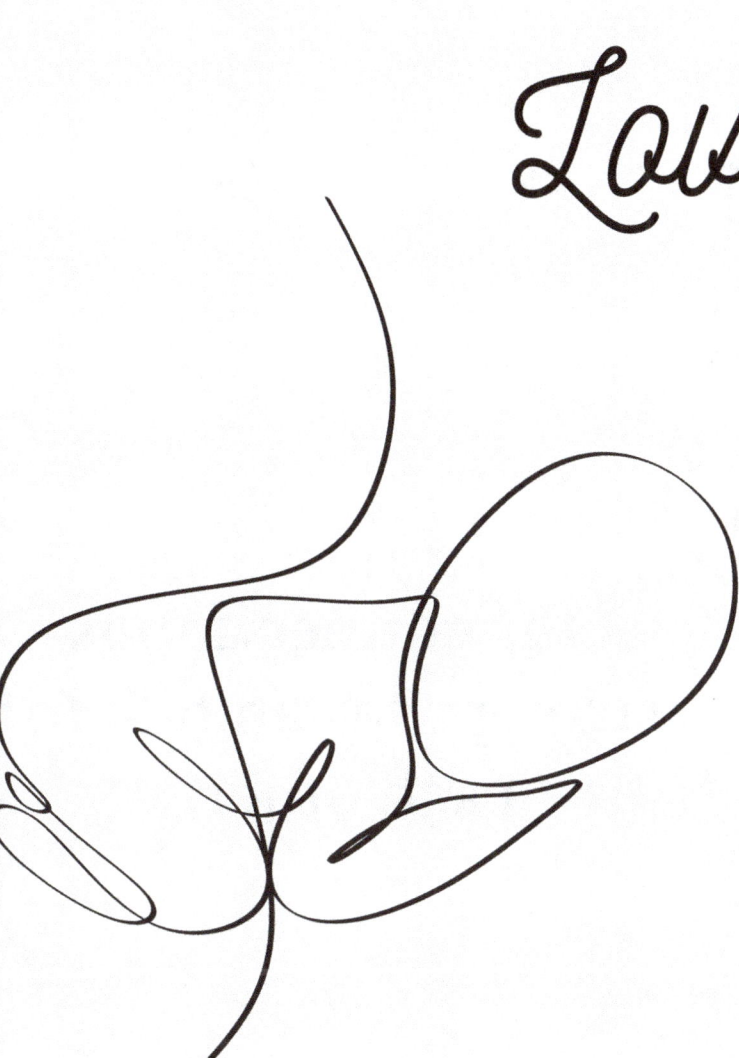

My Magical Baby,

I have loved you from the time I knew you were growing in my belly.

You are a part of me and now that I am carrying you,

My love for you is so deep that I can touch and feel you.

Our connection is strong: we can talk to each other.

When I say "I love you," something within me leaps.

It's a feeling you will one day soon have with me.

Responsibility

Now that I have you to care for, I have become much more responsible about what I do.

I know that everything I do can affect you while you are inside of me.

That is why I make sure to get enough rest so that you can have enough rest and grow.

I make sure to eat nutritious meals like colorful fruits and vegetables so you can grow healthy in my belly.

I drink enough water to stay hydrated, for both you and me.

I exercise to stay physically strong so that you can become strong within my womb.

Self-Image

You are my child, I love every inch of you with all my heart.

From the moment you were conceived, to this very moment, I see how much you are growing by the size of my belly.

I love looking at myself in the mirror just to look at you and see how much you are growing as the day goes by.

Because of you I have a glow that reflects in my skin, causing my skin to become so bright and beautiful.

Faith

You and I were hand-picked for each other.

Your arrival is a message to the world that God has a perfect plan and purpose for you.
He will reveal it as you grow, it is written into your DNA.

You have greatness within you and this world needs it!

I can't wait to see who you will grow up to become.

Protection

I will protect you, my precious baby.
The world can sometimes be a cold and
mean place.

But you don't have to worry.
I will be here to protect and shield you
from this world.

Each day I will pray for protection as our
Heavenly Father keeps you safe.

Attitude

I can tell how my attitude affects your attitude.

Because of this, I try my best to remain positive in any circumstance.

My days are not always happy days, but you inspire me to keep a positive attitude.

I keep a positive attitude because of how it can affect you.

I don't want to see you upset.

14

After all, you're the only one
who knows what my heart
sounds like from the inside.

Magical Baby

You are

Beautiful
Loved
Greatness
Appreciated
Wanted
Accepted

My blessing and an answer to my prayer.

I am awaiting your arrival.

Love, Your Mommy

"Before I formed you in the womb I knew you, before you were born I
set you apart; I appointed you as a prophet to the nation."

Jeremiah 1:5

A few ways to relax while bonding with your baby:

Sing lullabies and talk to your unborn baby. Your growing baby's hearing is developing from as early as 15 weeks, they can enjoy the daily soundtrack of your heartbeat.

Go for a walk

Try taking some time out to bond with your bump by going for a walk. It's great exercise and easy to fit into your daily routine, even if you are working.

Enjoy a bath with your growing baby.

A nice long soak is a perfect way to get away from it all and enjoy some me time. It's also a great chance to devote some attention to your growing baby. Just make sure the water is at the right temperature.

Try antenatal yoga

Antenatal yoga class is a fantastic way to relax and help you focus on the amazing work that your body is doing and pay attention to your growing baby.

Respond to your unborn baby's kicks

You may start to feel your baby's movements from about 18 weeks. Feeling your growing baby move can be wonderfully reassuring after weeks of having no idea of what's going on in there.

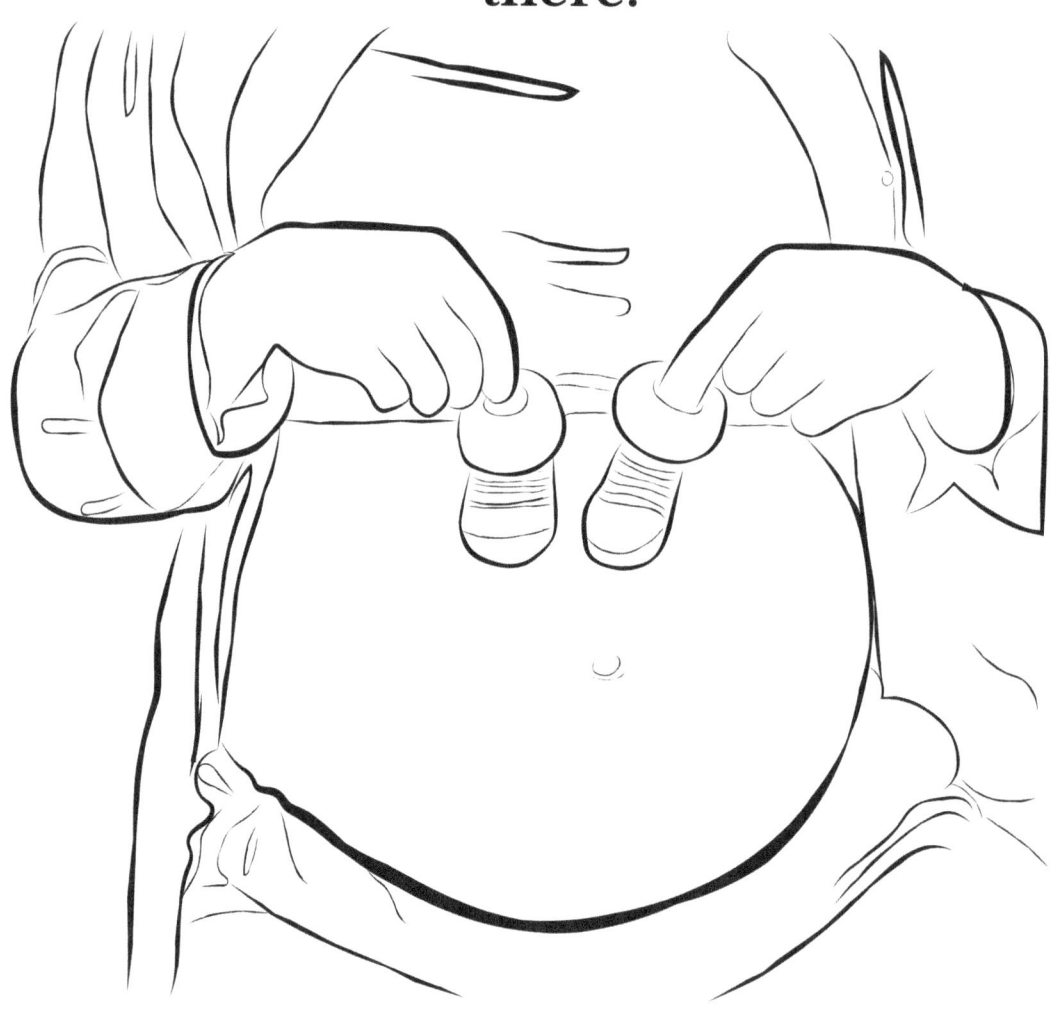

Get dad involved

It's not just you who wants to develop a lasting bond with your baby – dad-to-be will want to get involved as well! When you feel the baby kick, have him place his hand over your tummy so that he can feel the movements too.

Congratulations on your pregnancy!

The beginning of human life is a beautiful experience. There is nothing else like it. As a mother, you want to establish a relationship with your baby in the womb before your "magical baby" makes their grand entrance into the world.

"Magical Baby" consists of simple words and detailed illustrations that invite mothers to affirm their baby's uniqueness. It connects a mother's thoughts to her baby's heart before physically laying eyes on each other. God blessed you with a "magical baby."

"You saw me before I was born. Every day of my life was recorded in your book. Every moment was laid out before a single day had passed. Psalms 139:16 NLT

About the Author

Best-selling author Dieuna Chrispin has been working with children for nearly a decade. She is an educator, workshop presenter, and director of her own family childcare center. She resides in Palm Beach County, with her husband Luther, and their three children.